Keeper of Limits

Keeper of Limits

The Mrs. Cavendish Poems

Stephen Dunn

Quarternote Chapbook Series #12

Sarabande  Books

LOUISVILLE , KENTUCKY

FIRST EDITION

Library of Congress Cataloging-in-Publication Data

Dunn, Stephen, 1939–
  [Poems. Selections]
  The keeper of limits : the Mrs. Cavendish poems / Stephen Dunn.
    pages ; cm. — (Quarternote chapbook series ; #12)
  ISBN 978-1-941411-11-7 (pbk. : alk. paper)
  I. Title.
  PS3554.U49A6 2015
  811'.54—dc23
                         2015004391

Cover design by Kristen Radtke.
Interior layout and composition by Kirkby Gann Tittle.

Manufactured in Canada.

This book is printed on acid-free paper.

Sarabande Books is a nonprofit literary organization.

The Kentucky Arts Council, the state arts agency, supports Sarabande Books with state tax dollars and federal funding from the National Endowment for the Arts.

CONTENTS

Acknowledgments

Five Points: "Mrs. Cavendish and the American Dilemma," "Mrs. Cavendish and the End of Secrecy," "Mrs. Cavendish and the General Malaise," "Mrs. Cavendish and the Dancer," and "Mrs. Cavendish and the Learning Curve"

The Georgia Review: "Rachel Becomes Mrs. Cavendish," "The Young Mrs. Cavendish," "Mrs. Cavendish's Politics," "Mrs. Cavendish Speaks," "Mrs. Cavendish and the Democracy Game," and "Mrs. Cavendish Becomes the Real Thing"

Harper's: "Mrs. Cavendish and the General Malaise" (chose from *Five Points*)

Plume: "Mrs. Cavendish, Hope, and Other Four Letter Words"

Rachel Becomes Mrs. Cavendish

She moved into his name
willingly, for reasons phonetically
and otherwise obvious.
She especially liked that Cavendish
had a ring of entitlement to it
among bankers and brokers
in the New Jersey suburbs
where they moved to escape
her friends, and join his.
She was young, and had a sense
of what could be called waspy fun.
She'd never met anyone like him.
Both of them kept me off balance in those days.
When I'd visit I'd find myself half-beguiled,
half-annoyed, by how she'd tell lies
about things we'd experienced together.
But what could I do? She was in the act
of becoming Mrs. Cavendish, and I knew
from then on I'd keep her past
in the same closed-up closet
where I kept my own dark secrets.
In that way her husband and I became
keepers of her preferred memories.
He knew I loved her, but thought of me
as an adoring remnant, essentially prehistoric.
The truth is always different
from what anyone says out loud,
but who really cares? Not I, said the man
I chose to be, nor I nor I nor I—
among the many of us she left teetering.

The Young Mrs. Cavendish

Because back then she accepted
almost any problem as the normal state of things
she thought the homeless and the affluent
were just part of the landscape, inevitable as storms

and sunsets. It was easy, she said, such thinking,
and when it wasn't, it simply wasn't. I felt like
disavowing her right there, but I rarely knew
what to do in her presence,

found it hard to resist the lilt of her voice,
her blithe carelessness. When she began to use the word
spiritual as if it were something you could study for,
like citizenship, I should have collapsed into laughter.

Let's embrace our ignorance, I finally said to her,
half-aware I was revealing my own brand of sanctimony.
I remembered for both of us how pleased she was
when we discussed Ayn Rand and free enterprise,

and those years she instructed others in the art
of selfishness. Let the poor work harder,
she'd say, let the strong get stronger. She'd cite
Howard Roark as her man of the hour, would tell

anyone who'd listen that Adam Smith eats Marx
for breakfast. Then she went to college, and there
was the world, fraught with complications
of competing ideas. Now she says

she was an idiot, hadn't yet tripped over herself
in pursuit of an idea, or lost a job, or had to rely
on the kindness of the unambitious. It took forever
before she could separate the shit from the shinola.

Mrs. Cavendish's Lament

I was good all day and did what I was supposed to.

Mrs. Cavendish's Politics

Because she came to believe that everyone
had the right to be heard, but not necessarily
the right to be taken seriously, she was trusted
by all sides. And, I, too, admired her,

but would argue that having so many friends
made her suspiciously indiscriminate.
"Well," Mrs. Cavendish said, "I don't
like you very much, does that count?"

Taken aback, but at the same time pleased,
I told her I was suspect too, an atheist
libertine coward, and often called my actions
mature when in fact I was playing things safe.

And this was how, after many years apart,
Mrs. Cavendish and I became friends again,
real friends, telling each the semblance
of truth, always holding just enough back.

Mrs. Cavendish and the Period of Mourning

Mr. Cavendish was William to his friends, Billy
to Rachel, a name she gave him in the sweet
early days of their courtship. After a few years,
things quieted into the various hums
of marriage. They spoke and suffered politely,
house and what-shall-we-have-for-dinner talk
replacing *baby, baby, oh baby.* By the time
Mr. Cavendish's car caromed off that guard rail
and spun into traffic, they had achieved the normal.

Nevertheless Rachel mourned his absence,
now and then turning to me for something
to lean on, which I gave with a hidden gratitude.
For a long while I turned her sighs into stories,
yet welcomed when she started to laugh again,
freeing me from grieving what I had no heart for.
Mrs. Cavendish, I said to myself, I'm happy
and hopeful, but of course no one could hear me.

Mrs. Cavendish's Dog

I'm a dead dog for real now;
no longer can I rise
from my fakery, alert to commands
I'd come to think of as love,
though I never did obey
as well as Sundown did,
or as a truly good dog would.
To play the slave, not be one,
was my code. You understood,
who would play the master.
From my grave in the yard,
Mrs. Cavendish, I see now
you had no gift for it, or heart.
Bad dog, you'd say,
so little conviction in your voice.
In seconds you'd be patting my head.
Forgiveness made you happy; I'd tip
over trash cans to be forgiven by you.
Let me tell you it's no life being dead.
I'd give anything to chase the gulls again.
But clarities come when the body goes.
For whatever it's worth, you should know—
you who think so much—
only what's been smelled or felt
gets remembered. And in the dark earth
no doors open, no one ever comes home.

Mrs. Cavendish and the Winter Guide

It's snowing, Mrs. Cavendish, maybe not yet
where you are, but here it's coming down rabbits
and golf balls, and at this moment a group
of tall albinos is convening on my lawn.
Let me be your hyperbolic winter guide,
and I'll have you forget what weathermen say
about worry and gloom. How about, for starters,
a long, defiant slide down Death Mountain,
everyone cheering you on? Or can we drive
to a mostly frozen lake, lace up,
and do figure eights where the soft spots are?
Or, if you prefer to stay inside, I'm a stay-inside guy
too. I like quiet games in which no one can lose.
It's snowing harder now, Mrs. Cavendish,
the wet and heavy kind. Even with my bad back
you should know I want to shovel your walk,
risk a spasmodic attack to be closer to your door.
The forecast is everything that's happening to me
will soon happen to you. Do you like the way
that sounds? Think of it as the universe singing
my praises, all my mischief approved.
Mrs. Cavendish, it's blizzardy cold.
Come out anyway. Come out and play.
I've made a snow woman and dressed her
in bright scarves and with charcoal eyes,
but clearly she won't do. She smells wrong.
She's not you. From you what I need is a sign.
I have a key to the shed where there's some wood
and a wood-burning stove.
It's where we can dry off, change our clothes.

Mrs. Cavendish and the American Dilemma

Mrs. Cavendish, dear Mrs. Cavendish, I want
to say that though your husband was born
in England, you need not prove yourself American

by acquiring what you don't need. I've seen you
try to shop your way out of an impenetrable mood
at some cathedral of a mall, your small inheritance

dwindling day by day. I should rename you
Mrs. Conspicuous Consumption, she who
takes herself to the cleaners, and doesn't know

the cost. Prodigious, Mrs. Cavendish,
that's what you are. You told me once (in a weak
moment) you'd like to slow dance with me

to music only we could hear, inner melodies
so much ours you'd feel the beginnings
of something hard saying hello to your thigh.

That's all I think about now, a rising up
from almost nothing, my American dream.
Mrs. Cavendish, if it would please you

I'd lie down with you on one of those flat beds
that carries big merchandise at Home Depot,
then have someone roll us over to Walmart

or Staples, those giants that have swallowed
the little guys who once made the neighborhood
a neighborhood, and called me by name.

Maybe there's no connection between the demise
of Jack's Hardware and why so many hate us,
though I worry that to lie down with you

will activate those crazies on the lookout
for the likes of us, their backpacks
filled with motives and zeal.

I oppose and sympathize with their hatred,
but would be happy if a few of them
were hanged. It's so difficult to desire someone

and be principled, too. America the beautiful
some people sing, able to believe all the words.
Mrs. Cavendish, I'm trying. I'm trying for you.

Mrs. Cavendish and the End of Secrecy

Morning and the moon still out,
a fuzzy moodiness over the land
as the sea struggles with that old
magnetism from above. Mrs. Cavendish,
the sea doesn't want to be bothered today;
it merely wishes to behave like a lake,
reflect back a face like its own,
sometimes wild, mostly calm.
It also would like to change
its salty ways, but like you,
Mrs. Cavendish, it can't—
                the world is various
but also cruel. I tell you, Mr. Cavendish,
you should buy a big flat screen TV and engage
the world in the safe way most of us do.
When the census man comes with his charts
and those categories he'll want you to check,
remember to lie about your age. Tell him
you're not happy about the end of secrecy,
you don't want to become a stat.
                At another time
the sea, too, will want to undulate and roar,
not be lake-like at all. Mrs. Cavendish,
there's so much whim and peculiarity
to accommodate. I wish I could tell you
the best stroke to use if you choose to swim
where the orcas rule. All I know
is that you shouldn't answer if a man
without a heart asks about yours.
He'll have plans, he'll have strange eyes

in the front of his head. They'll be for you.
And soon the moon will recede, cannot help,
will only serve as witness, as the cosmos does.

Mrs. Cavendish and the Dancer

Mrs. Cavendish desired the man in the fedora
who danced the tarantella without regard
for who might care. All her life she had
a weakness for abandon, and, when the music
stopped, for anyone who could turn a phrase.
The problem was Mrs. Cavendish wanted it all
to mean something in a world crazed and splattered
with the gook of apparent significance.
The dancer studied philosophy, she told me,
knew the difference between a sophist
and a sophomore, despite my insistence
that hardly any existed. It seemed that everyone
but she knew that sadness awaits the needy.
Mr. Cavendish, too, when he was alive,
could be equally naive, might invite a wolf
in man's clothing to spend a night
at their house. This was how she
mythologized her husband—a man of what
she called honor, no sense of marital danger,
scrupled beyond all scrupulosity.
The tarantella man was gorgeous and oily,
and, let's forgive her, Mrs. Cavendish
was lonely. His hair slicked back, he didn't
resemble her deceased in the slightest,
which in the half-light of memory's belittered
passageways made her ga-ga. And I, as ever,
would cajole and warn, hoping history
and friendship might be on my side.
Mrs. Cavendish, I'd implore, lie down
with this dandy if it feels good, but, please,
when he smells most of sweetness, get a grip,
develop a gripe, try to breathe your own air.

Mrs. Cavendish and the General Malaise

Like a boxer at a pre-fight weigh-in, defiant,
no sign of acceptance, Mrs. Cavendish began
to stare meaninglessness in the eye.
The difference: no one, nothing, stared back.
Mrs. Cavendish, I said, it's impossible to win.
As we consider today, it's almost tomorrow.
As we admire the flowers, how easily they're ravaged
by wind and rain. The best we can hope for
is a big, fat novel, slowing down the course of time.
Several tomorrows always linger in the margins,
which means until the very last page
you'll choose to live with the raw evidence
of how someone else sees and makes a world.
Mrs. Cavendish, I'm also sorry to report
the maps are missing from the office of
How to Get Where You Want To Go—
just one more symptom of the general malaise.
I have little hope that they can be found,
at least not in our lifetime. At the risk of telling you
what you already know, Mrs. Cavendish, here's
something merely true: the insufficiency of the moon
has been replaced by the lantern, the lantern by
the light bulb, but what won't go away is the promise
of salvation out there in the bright beyond.
There will always be people who think suffering
leads to enlightenment, who place themselves
on the verge of what's about to break, or go
dangerously wrong. Let's resist them
and their thinking, you and I. Let's not rush
toward that sure thing that awaits us,
which can dumb us into nonsense and pain.

My dog keeps one eye open when he sleeps.
My cat prefers your house where the mice are.
Stare ahead, my friend. The whole world is on alert.
Mrs. Cavendish, every day is old news.

Mrs. Cavendish's Dream

I had spoken to her, she said, from some far away
unidentifiable place, and I was all mouth,
three times the size of any mouth
she'd ever seen. It was a mouth that didn't want
to suck or kiss so the dream didn't seem sexual,
nor did it want to devour, thus she was not fearful.
The mouth only seemed to want to speak
and be heard, and right before she woke
she remembered thinking she wished it was an ear,
a giant ear that would encourage her to say and say
and say. The next day on the telephone,
she concluded the mouth had all the vatic
and pontifical qualities of a poet's mouth, and probably
was mine. Did it speak? I asked. And if it did,
what did it say?, always searching for giveaways
that might indicate what she thought of me.
If you want to live in the wilderness, make sure
you know the difference between ordinary shit
and the scat of grizzlies, is what the mouth said.
Then before she fell back to sleep, the mouth added
something like, *Let's return to zero.*
Mrs. Cavendish—I was laughing as I spoke—
I think you made that up. No, she said, it's all true,
except maybe the third "say," which was irresistible.

Mrs. Cavendish and the Outlaw

The cross-dresser, the albino, the man who once had legs,
and so many others out there displaying their otherness—
Mrs. Cavendish, how long it took us to recognize they want
what we want, and how they must struggle. Some are brave,
many just silly or stupid, as we have been, and stumble
into daylight like things that have always lived underground.
To wish to be loved, and not be able to see where you're going—
oh Mrs Cavendish, you know what I'm talking about.
So difficult for us to exit the mirrorless rooms we grew up in.
So difficult to know the dark, brotherly other in ourselves.

I do know, however, it's easy to take a false step
by standing still, or to cling to a single identity.
But I'm not sure if I'm brave or deprived enough
to be an outlaw. Are you, Mrs. Cavendish?
Once I was asked to believe in a radiant goodness.
Had I been given another choice—something
that spoke to the life I lived—I might have a prayer
a bad boy could say with conviction. Mrs. Cavendish,
I don't. I can only imagine the words floating, unspoken.

Mrs. Cavendish Speaks

Don't get me wrong, I'm occasionally grateful
for my friend's advice, but sometimes
he doesn't understand that the rational
separates this from that, leaves behind
more than it can combine, or make sense of.
Truth is, I simply don't want
the world he wants. Give me the unfilled
space between hunger and the morsel
it can't quite reach, or between taste
and the after taste that's remembered
and therefore forever sought.
I want my sense of sense to be uncooperative,
the way the truly sensual self-interested is.
And while I'm complaining, I wish ˙
he'd call me Rachel, as he did
in the old neighborhood
when he'd dribble his basketball
in front of my house to get my attention.
Maybe it's because I always gave him
less than he craves that the formality
of Mrs. Cavendish exists between us.
Maybe he believed marriage changes who a person is.
And who knows, maybe it does and did.
I became Mrs. Cavendish to him,
perhaps because he needed that distance.
But after my husband died, I think I've become
Rachel again. I know quite well the follies
of the sensual are similar
to the follies of the logical,
and have learned to be wary of both.

Yet I want to say, Oh my dear friend,
just because I don't listen is no reason
for you to stop saying what you must.

Mrs. Cavendish and the Learning Curve

Mrs. Cavendish was aware of the tick
of the clock, the seemingly often unseemly
progress of time, but knew little of the now,
which was known to go backward, or pick up
where it left off. We'd argue about such matters,
affectionately, because she knew I trusted her
mindful instincts, as much as I knew
she tolerated mine. Death shows no favoritism,
she once said, and added that history
was a strangely beautiful graveyard
where the poor lie down with the rich.
But in general Mrs. Cavendish
loved the enigmas of happenstance
more than any slippage toward certainty,
and the truth-teller in her loved
as if more than *this is so.*
It was easy to be fond of this person
she had become, her heart often ascending
to where her mind presided,
properly warming what got spoken.
I marveled at how she could disturb
wisdom with the gentlest of doubts,
but also worried that she couldn't commit
to any one thing. One evening I said,
Mrs. Cavendish, I'm afraid you need something
to give your whole self to, or maybe some rules
for getting to a place inescapable,
some place not in between.
How then would I stay alive? she said.

Mrs. Cavendish Speaks of the Unforgivable

More than once I've permitted in myself
what I wouldn't forgive in others.

Mrs. Cavendish Returns From Inner Space

She hardly knew she'd been gone, so familiar
and comfortably odd the atmosphere had seemed
to her. She'd been inhabiting herself, feeding off
of what she'd accumulated over the years—the sweet
and the bittersweet—in search of the real Cavendish.
She said she'd been in the land of whispers
and secrets, the sun now and then breaking through
cloud cover to form her particular universe,
sometimes fraught, sometimes serene.
Mrs. Cavendish, I said, I'm glad to have you back,
looking so svelt and ready for what
the world must still have in store for you.
She lived a while with the answers, she reported,
which questioned and doubted themselves,
everything temporary and fixed, then temporary again.
Nothing was in store for her, nothing at all.
And I, who had kept watch as she disappeared
and returned—often without moving a muscle—
wanted to say to her that here in the brightness
of her kitchen, among the unquestionable
silverware, the certainty of the four walls around us,
I was hurt a little but not surprised
that she seemed not to need—prematurely
I felt—what always I had given her.

Mrs. Cavendish Comes to Terms

When she was alone, she said, everything and everyone—
the streets she walked, the people she passed,
even the birds in the trees—also seemed alone.
At home, she'd avoid mirrors and their keen accuracies,
     and, once, when I called on her, she asked
what I saw when I turned the light on in a darkened room—
the dark illuminated, or just less dark? Were the bones
of the room suddenly aglow?
     Mrs. Cavendish, I said, you sound depressed,
you should look for someone poorly trained—they abound—
and make an appointment without intention
of keeping it. In other words, be like me—
     a gesture toward, no actual fessing up.
I was pleased that she smiled, and took it as a sign
we were on the same blank page, had mutual ways
of fooling ourselves. Mrs. Cavendish, what shall we do
     if we can't have the fine loneliness lovers have,
their arms encircling what is so tentatively theirs?
Shall we kick some cans up and down the street,
fill the emptiness with cacophonous clangs?

Strange comforts are not what I want, she said.

Mrs. Cavendish, Hope, and Other Four-Letter Words

Mrs. Cavendish, let's continue, out of habit, to expect
from death a tiny leniency, and when it arrives
let's see if we can choose the transport of our choice.
Not an airplane, of course, but something that might
descend at a speed slow enough to keep up
from what can spoil the illusion of a good time.
Maybe even a vehicle that doesn't move.

But let's not count on it.
Hope, Mrs. Cavendish, is a four letter word.
Have a little fun, that's all. Wear your hair
in Medusa curls, and turn a few onlookers into stone.
Or like a caterpillar begin to undress, do a little
twirl and a shrug, and emerge as something else.
In the meantime, I'll stay around, an itch in my heart,
sleeping in a different room. Hope it. Hope it all.

Mrs. Cavendish and the Beyond

Beyond the mountain peak, a roundish glowing thing
was in some early stage of becoming itself, or was it
a helium-filled balloon on its way to a metropolis?

I couldn't tell, but we both saw it from her porch,
and uttered a collective *Look!* then got quiet
for a moment or two and just stared.

It's merely an alien ship from another world,
Mrs. Cavendish finally said, with the confidence
of a woman who'd gone far, albeit only in books,

toward expertise on such matters. As usual,
I was suspicious of what I called *easy mysticism*,
and wondered if it were a new schtick of hers,

or had she been, for years, following the advice
in the *I Ching* or from fortune cookies? I feared
she might be suffering from a case of innocence.

But suddenly the balloon or whatever it was
seemed threatening, as if it were about to descend
or explode in mid-air, moving as if out of control

or being controlled by a foreign force. Every machine
will break down at some point—I knew that—but is
also susceptible to tyranny, which made me think

about how many people might want to get back at us
for the use of bombs and drones in the name
of goodness and our way of life. Mrs. Cavendish, I said,

you're thinking interplanetary, and I hope you're right,
but international would be more worrisome, wouldn't it?
As far as I know, we haven't hurt anyone on the moon,

haven't taken out a village on Mars or Jupiter.
But just then the thing sped away
over the mountain, as if its mission was a desire

to become a memory, and had been completed.

Mrs. Cavendish and the Democracy Game

We were watching television, my hand
on your thigh, and I wanted you to pay
special attention to that senator on the screen—
how good he was at voicing public outrage
at the deceit he'd mastered in back rooms.

See, I said, that's how the game is played;
you seek consensus, but only after
you've twisted the necessary arms.
I remember you looked at me strangely, as if
I were advocating instead of pointing out.

I went on to say, Mrs. Cavendish, it's not
that I approve. I love to watch the possible
take shape. And I love to see it defeated too.
Sometimes all it takes is the simple truth,
someone actually saying what he means.

What makes you think, she said,
that I don't understand move and counter-move,
or, now, where your hand wishes to go?
Isn't politics the art of getting what you want?
Think higher of me, my friend. Higher, please.

Mrs. Cavendish and the Persistence of Desire

Evening becomes you, Mrs. Cavendish, because
that's when longing and possibility congeal,
become one, your black dress slit
up the side, and the cinematic way you glide
(in my mind) down long corridors
like that graceful woman in Marienbad—
only as I remember she was dressed in white,
diaphanous, her gait slow and apparently without
purpose, though at the end of one corridor is a man,
playing a game he can't lose, which other players
can't resist, and you're headed his way.
Someone is going to die, I'm going to make sure
not you, because this dream, this movie
is mine now, and I want to go as far as I can
into it, beyond any affirmation or certainty,
to a place where you can neither accept nor refuse,
you whom I ask once again to give up your name.

Mrs. Cavendish and the Keeper of Limits

She would often seek that splendid rush,
not caring that it would soon subside.

After all, the issue was joy; she knew
it was never meant to last. Disappointment

was always nearby. She couldn't make
it disappear, or entirely ignore it,

but once she discovered the freedoms
within boundaries, it was like living

with a difficult but fair father, something
to push against while you found your own way.

Mrs. Cavendish, I said, I'm on your side. Like you,
I abhor the pretty good, the okay—those enemies

of wonderment. I want everything that's mine,
she said, to rise, be contained, spill over.

Mrs. Cavendish Becomes the Real Thing

With the expectation of someone who has
succeeded more than once, Mrs. Cavendish
sits down each morning to engage the world.
Each day is a first day, and nothing is quite real
to her unless, finally, it bears her signature.
By the time she finishes breakfast, she's sure
that a well-made omelet falls under the category
of an intrinsic good, and is equally convinced
that the shape of a lemon is superior to that
of an orange—that beauty, if symmetrical,
is one of the enemies of improvisation.

She reads a little before she attempts a sentence
of her own, vows never to use the word *God*
because she's read that it's a word
that frightens God, makes Him go away.
But Mrs. Cavendish can't help but blaspheme
her own tenets, and, besides, believes a God
that isn't here can't be a God that goes away.
She writes, *Give me a steady authentic flame*
that lights the way home, and says it to me over the phone.

I tell her I love the line, but the fact is
the smarter Mrs. Cavendish gets the more I recede.
Even her silences bring news that is news
to me, a strange accuracy in the ways they shape
how I feel. Like now. Like sure-to-be tomorrow.

I don't know what else to say, except *hello*
Mrs. Cavendish, hello from afar.

Mrs. Cavendish and the Man Left Behind

Without power, among the sunken skipped stones and shipwrecks,
I heard the wind taking ownership of the trees, and rowed
without purpose, neither weakened nor strengthened
by hope or despair. Last week, I could see beaver dams
upriver and other signs of natural trouble, but I pledged to keep going,
waterway after waterway, until you were found.

But of course, Mrs. Cavendish, you could be dead by now,
and the spot where your skiff went down
will never be known. But you could also be somewhere
hanging on, maybe to a log, waiting for me, or some sailor
in search of a mermaid you'd become if you could.
I've read about a lotus that survived

at the bottom of a lake for twelve hundred years,
then sprouted again, and coconuts that would float
across an ocean, wash ashore, and take root.
Maybe you're in a hotel room with the man who helped
you fake ruin. He's ordering from room service French toast
for two, blueberries and cream.

And your name, is it the same? And what do you want?
When someday you're discovered alive, I hope you'll find
this note I'm leaving at the dock with old master of jibs
and slips who knew us when. He'll know where I am.
You see, I've thought of everything,
the way a man left behind does, Rachel my love.

STEPHEN DUNN is the author of seventeen collections of poetry, most recently *Lines of Defense* (2013), *Here and Now* (2011), and *What Goes On: Selected & New Poems: 1995–2009. Different Hours* won the Pulitzer Prize in 2001, and *Loosestrife* was a National Book Critics Circle Award finalist in 1996. His other awards include: the Academy Award in Literature from The American Academy of Arts & Letters, The Paterson Award for Sustained Literary Achievement, Fellowships from the Guggenheim and Rockefeller Foundations, three NEA Creative Writing Fellowships, the Levinson and Oscar Blumenthal Prizes from *Poetry*, and many others. He is Distinguished Professor (emeritus) of Creative Writing at Richard Stockton College of New Jersey, and has also taught at Columbia University, NYU, University of Michigan, Princeton, and the University of Washington. He spends most of his time these days in Frostburg, Maryland where he lives with his wife, the writer Barbara Hurd.

Sarabande Books is a nonprofit literary press located in Louisville, KY and Brooklyn, NY. Founded in 1994 to champion poetry, short fiction, and essay, we are committed to creating lasting editions that honor exceptional writing. For more information, please visit sarabandebooks.org.